© 2020 by Ruth Buchanan

All rights reserved. No part of this book may be reproduced in any form by any electronic or mechanical means including photocopying, recording, or information storage and retrieval without permission in writing from the author except in the case of brief quotations embodied in critical articles or reviews.

Cover design and interior formatting by TK Consulting & Design, LLC.

Author photo © 2016 by Rita DeCassia Photography

Published by Build a Better Us

THE CROSS IN THE CULTURE:
CONNECTING OUR STORIES TO THE GREATEST STORY EVER TOLD

THE WORKBOOK

RUTH BUCHANAN

Introduction

This workbook accompanies *The Cross in the Culture: Connecting Our Stories to the Greatest Story Ever Told*. Here you will find discussion questions intended to maximize personal study and further group discussions. If this workbook somehow made it into your hands before you've read the book, you will still get something out of these exercises. To enjoy the full experience, read *The Cross in the Culture* first.

Better Together

In God's plan, we all need one another. In analyzing stories, we benefit from each other's voices, perspectives, and wisdom. In the spirit of *The Cross in the Culture*, this workbook provides a framework for you, your family, your friends, or your small group to come together and engage your faith with cultural artifacts. You can discuss movies,

The Cross in the Culture: The Workbook

books, documentaries, or TV shows. Plays, musicals, radio dramas, and podcast episodes work, too!

To enjoy a truly communal event, set aside time to experience a story together. This might be a short story read aloud by one member of the group or a movie/episode screened together and discussed immediately afterward. You could subject old favorites to fresh perspectives or come together to experience a new release.

Of course, due to considerations of timing or distance, you may not be able to meet in person for the entire exercise. You may choose to consume the story separately, prepare your notes, and meet for a discussion over snacks and drinks. You may connect through screens. Either way, the more communal you're able to make this experience, the more everyone will benefit.

Be careful not to leave anyone behind. Consider the needs of all members in the group when making your selections. If it's a book, make sure it's still in print and widely available. If it's a movie or show, check that it's accessible to everyone. Depending on your group, you may need to confirm that closed captions are available for the hearing impaired, that audio descriptions can be accessed for the

The Cross in the Culture: The Workbook

visually impaired, that language levels in the story are suitable for ESL/EFL learners, and so forth.

My prayer is that together, we will all be better equipped to bring faith to bear on the stories we consume. That includes the movies we love, the books we only read because our friends forced us, and everything in between. May we recognize the shared characteristics of our humanity. May we witness in every story the transcendent glory of the Triune God. May we connect every story to the greatest story ever told.

The Cross in the Culture: The Workbook

NAME OF THE STORY: _____

| **Date read/ Screened** | **Story medium** (book, short story, movie, etc) |

MEMBERS PRESENT FOR DISCUSSION

_____   _____

_____   _____

_____   _____

_____   _____

DISCUSSION **QUESTIONS**

1. What genres would this story fall under? List all that apply.

The Cross in the Culture: The Workbook

_____

_____

_____

2. In light of what was discussed about genres in *The Cross in the Culture*, does anything about this story stand out differently to you?

_____

_____

_____

3. What are some major world events currently unfolding in the news? In what ways do these events either tie into the story or affect the way you think about the plot points, development, or specific story elements?

_____

_____

_____

4. What does this story reveal about basic longings of the human heart?

_____

_____

The Cross in the Culture: The Workbook

_____

5. In your opinion, how does this story tell the truth?

_____

_____

_____

_____

6. In your opinion, are there any ways in which this story does not tell the truth?

_____

_____

_____

7. If the storyteller were sitting here among you, what questions would you ask? What praise would you offer? What pushback?

_____

_____

_____

_____

_____

The Cross in the Culture: The Workbook

_____

8. Does the story give glory to the Triune God overtly or covertly? Describe how. Does this seem to be intentional on the storyteller's part?

_____

_____

_____

9. Who in the story demonstrates actions or character qualities that remind you of Christ? of an anti-Christ?

_____

_____

_____

10. What bridges can we build from this story to the gospel?

_____

_____

_____

11. Are there any questions you would like to raise with the group?

The Cross in the Culture: The Workbook

_____
_____
_____

The Cross in the Culture: The Workbook

NOTES

The Cross in the Culture: The Workbook

NAME OF THE STORY: _____

Date read/ Screened

Story medium
(book, short story, movie, etc)

MEMBERS PRESENT FOR DISCUSSION

_____ _____

_____ _____

_____ _____

_____ _____

DISCUSSION **QUESTIONS**

1. What genres would this story fall under? List all that apply.

_____

The Cross in the Culture: The Workbook

_____

_____

2. In light of what was discussed about genres in *The Cross in the Culture*, does anything about this story stand out differently to you?

_____

_____

_____

3. What are some major world events currently unfolding in the news? In what ways do these events either tie into the story or affect the way you think about the plot points, development, or specific story elements?

_____

_____

_____

4. What does this story reveal about basic longings of the human heart?

_____

_____

The Cross in the Culture: The Workbook

_____

_____

5. In your opinion, how does this story tell the truth?

_____

_____

_____

6. In your opinion, are there any ways in which this story does not tell the truth?

_____

_____

_____

7. If the storyteller were sitting here among you, what questions would you ask? What praise would you offer? What pushback?

_____

_____

_____

The Cross in the Culture: The Workbook

8. Does the story give glory to the Triune God overtly or covertly? Describe how. Does this seem to be intentional on the storyteller's part?

   _____

   _____

   _____

9. Who in the story demonstrates actions or character qualities that remind you of Christ? of an anti-Christ?

   _____

   _____

   _____

10. What bridges can we build from this story to the gospel?

    _____

    _____

    _____

11. Are there any questions you would like to raise with the group?

    _____

    _____

The Cross in the Culture: The Workbook

_____
_____
_____

The Cross in the Culture: The Workbook

NOTES

The Cross in the Culture: The Workbook

NAME OF THE STORY: _____

| **Date read/ Screened** | **Story medium** (book, short story, movie, etc) |

MEMBERS PRESENT FOR DISCUSSION

_____   _____

_____   _____

_____   _____

_____   _____

DISCUSSION QUESTIONS

1. In light of what was discussed about genres in *The Cross in the Culture*, does anything about this story stand out differently to you?

The Cross in the Culture: The Workbook

_____

_____

_____

2. What are some major world events currently unfolding in the news? In what ways do these events either tie into the story or affect the way you think about the plot points, development, or specific story elements?

_____

_____

_____

3. What does this story reveal about basic longings of the human heart?

_____

_____

_____

4. In your opinion, how does this story tell the truth?

_____

_____

_____

The Cross in the Culture: The Workbook

5. In your opinion, are there any ways in which this story does not tell the truth?

_____
_____
_____

6. If the storyteller were sitting here among you, what questions would you ask? What praise would you offer? What pushback?

_____
_____
_____

7. Does the story give glory to the Triune God overtly or covertly? Describe how. Does this seem to be intentional on the storyteller's part?

_____
_____
_____

8. Who in the story demonstrates actions or character qualities that remind you of Christ? of an anti-Christ?

The Cross in the Culture: The Workbook

_____

_____

_____

9. What bridges can we build from this story to the gospel?

_____

_____

_____

10. Are there any questions you would like to raise with the group?

_____

_____

_____

_____

The Cross in the Culture: The Workbook

NOTES

The Cross in the Culture: The Workbook

NAME OF THE STORY: _____

Date read/ Screened

Story medium
(book, short story, movie, etc)

MEMBERS PRESENT FOR DISCUSSION

_____   _____
_____   _____
_____   _____
_____   _____

DISCUSSION **QUESTIONS**

The Cross in the Culture: The Workbook

1. In light of what was discussed about genres in *The Cross in the Culture*, does anything about this story stand out differently to you?

   _____

   _____

   _____

2. What are some major world events currently unfolding in the news? In what ways do these events either tie into the story or affect the way you think about the plot points, development, or specific story elements?

   _____

   _____

   _____

3. What does this story reveal about basic longings of the human heart?

   _____

   _____

   _____

4. In your opinion, how does this story tell the truth?

   _____

The Cross in the Culture: The Workbook

_____

_____

5. In your opinion, are there any ways in which this story does not tell the truth?

_____

_____

_____

6. If the storyteller were sitting here among you, what questions would you ask? What praise would you offer? What pushback?

_____

_____

_____

7. Does the story give glory to the Triune God overtly or covertly? Describe how. Does this seem to be intentional on the storyteller's part?

_____

_____

_____

The Cross in the Culture: The Workbook

8. Who in the story demonstrates actions or character qualities that remind you of Christ? of an anti-Christ?

_____

_____

_____

9. What bridges can we build from this story to the gospel?

_____

_____

_____

10. Are there any questions you would like to raise with the group?

_____

_____

_____

The Cross in the Culture: The Workbook

NOTES

The Cross in the Culture: The Workbook

NAME OF THE STORY: _____

Date read/ Screened

Story medium
(book, short story, movie, etc)

MEMBERS PRESENT FOR DISCUSSION

_____   _____

_____   _____

_____   _____

_____   _____

DISCUSSION **QUESTIONS**

1. In light of what was discussed about genres in *The Cross in the Culture*, does anything about this story stand out differently to you?

The Cross in the Culture: The Workbook

_____

_____

_____

2. What are some major world events currently unfolding in the news? In what ways do these events either tie into the story or affect the way you think about the plot points, development, or specific story elements?

_____

_____

_____

3. What does this story reveal about basic longings of the human heart?

_____

_____

_____

4. In your opinion, how does this story tell the truth?

_____

_____

_____

The Cross in the Culture: The Workbook

5. In your opinion, are there any ways in which this story does not tell the truth?

_____

_____

_____

6. If the storyteller were sitting here among you, what questions would you ask? What praise would you offer? What pushback?

_____

_____

_____

7. Does the story give glory to the Triune God overtly or covertly? Describe how. Does this seem to be intentional on the storyteller's part?

_____

_____

_____

8. Who in the story demonstrates actions or character qualities that remind you of Christ? of an anti-Christ?

_____

The Cross in the Culture: The Workbook

_____
_____

9. What bridges can we build from this story to the gospel?

_____
_____
_____

10. Are there any questions you would like to raise with the group?

_____
_____
_____
_____

The Cross in the Culture: The Workbook

NOTES

The Cross in the Culture: The Workbook

NAME OF THE STORY: _____

| **Date read/ Screened** | **Story medium** (book, short story, movie, etc) |

MEMBERS PRESENT FOR DISCUSSION

_____ _____
_____ _____
_____ _____
_____ _____

DISCUSSION **QUESTIONS**

1. In light of what was discussed about genres in *The Cross in the Culture*, does anything about this story stand out differently to you?

The Cross in the Culture: The Workbook

_____

_____

_____

2. What are some major world events currently unfolding in the news? In what ways do these events either tie into the story or affect the way you think about the plot points, development, or specific story elements?

_____

_____

_____

3. What does this story reveal about basic longings of the human heart?

_____

_____

_____

4. In your opinion, how does this story tell the truth?

_____

_____

_____

5. In your opinion, are there any ways in which this story does not tell the truth?

   _____
   _____
   _____

6. If the storyteller were sitting here among you, what questions would you ask? What praise would you offer? What pushback?

   _____
   _____
   _____

7. Does the story give glory to the Triune God overtly or covertly? Describe how. Does this seem to be intentional on the storyteller's part?

   _____
   _____
   _____

8. Who in the story demonstrates actions or character qualities that remind you of Christ? of an anti-Christ?

The Cross in the Culture: The Workbook

_____

_____

_____

9. What bridges can we build from this story to the gospel?

_____

_____

_____

10. Are there any questions you would like to raise with the group?

_____

_____

_____

The Cross in the Culture: The Workbook

NOTES

The Cross in the Culture: The Workbook

NAME OF THE STORY: _____

Date read/ Screened

Story medium
(book, short story, movie, etc)

MEMBERS PRESENT FOR DISCUSSION

_____   _____

_____   _____

_____   _____

_____   _____

DISCUSSION QUESTIONS

1. In light of what was discussed about genres in *The Cross in the Culture*, does anything about this story stand out differently to you?

The Cross in the Culture: The Workbook

_____

_____

_____

2. What are some major world events currently unfolding in the news? In what ways do these events either tie into the story or affect the way you think about the plot points, development, or specific story elements?

_____

_____

_____

_____

_____

3. What does this story reveal about basic longings of the human heart?

_____

_____

_____

4. In your opinion, how does this story tell the truth?

The Cross in the Culture: The Workbook

_____
_____
_____

5. In your opinion, are there any ways in which this story does not tell the truth?

_____
_____
_____

6. If the storyteller were sitting here among you, what questions would you ask? What praise would you offer? What pushback?

_____
_____
_____

7. Does the story give glory to the Triune God overtly or covertly? Describe how. Does this seem to be intentional on the storyteller's part?

_____
_____
_____

The Cross in the Culture: The Workbook

8. Who in the story demonstrates actions or character qualities that remind you of Christ? of an anti-Christ?

_____

_____

_____

9. What bridges can we build from this story to the gospel?

_____

_____

_____

10. Are there any questions you would like to raise with the group?

_____

_____

_____

The Cross in the Culture: The Workbook

NOTES

The Cross in the Culture: The Workbook

NAME OF THE STORY: _____

Date read/Screened

Story medium
(book, short story, movie, etc)

MEMBERS PRESENT FOR DISCUSSION

_____   _____

_____   _____

_____   _____

_____   _____

DISCUSSION QUESTIONS

1. In light of what was discussed about genres in *The Cross in the Culture*, does anything about this story stand out differently to you?

The Cross in the Culture: The Workbook

_____

_____

_____

2. What are some major world events currently unfolding in the news? In what ways do these events either tie into the story or affect the way you think about the plot points, development, or specific story elements?

_____

_____

_____

3. What does this story reveal about basic longings of the human heart?

_____

_____

_____

4. In your opinion, how does this story tell the truth?

_____

_____

_____

5. In your opinion, are there any ways in which this story does not tell the truth?

_____
_____
_____

6. If the storyteller were sitting here among you, what questions would you ask? What praise would you offer? What pushback?

_____
_____
_____

7. Does the story give glory to the Triune God overtly or covertly? Describe how. Does this seem to be intentional on the storyteller's part?

_____
_____
_____

8. Who in the story demonstrates actions or character qualities that remind you of Christ? of an anti-Christ?

The Cross in the Culture: The Workbook

_____
_____
_____

9. What bridges can we build from this story to the gospel?

_____
_____
_____

10. Are there any questions you would like to raise with the group?

_____
_____
_____

The Cross in the Culture: The Workbook

NOTES

The Cross in the Culture: The Workbook

NAME OF THE STORY: _____

| **Date read/ Screened** | **Story medium** (book, short story, movie, etc) |

MEMBERS PRESENT FOR DISCUSSION

_____   _____

_____   _____

_____   _____

_____   _____

DISCUSSION QUESTIONS

1. In light of what was discussed about genres in *The Cross in the Culture*, does anything about this story stand out differently to you?

The Cross in the Culture: The Workbook

_____
_____
_____

2. What are some major world events currently unfolding in the news? In what ways do these events either tie into the story or affect the way you think about the plot points, development, or specific story elements?

_____
_____
_____

3. What does this story reveal about basic longings of the human heart?

_____
_____
_____

4. In your opinion, how does this story tell the truth?

_____
_____
_____

The Cross in the Culture: The Workbook

5. In your opinion, are there any ways in which this story does not tell the truth?

_____

_____

_____

6. If the storyteller were sitting here among you, what questions would you ask? What praise would you offer? What pushback?

_____

_____

_____

7. Does the story give glory to the Triune God overtly or covertly? Describe how. Does this seem to be intentional on the storyteller's part?

_____

_____

_____

8. Who in the story demonstrates actions or character qualities that remind you of Christ? of an anti-Christ?

9. What bridges can we build from this story to the gospel?

10. Are there any questions you would like to raise with the group?

The Cross in the Culture: The Workbook

NOTES

The Cross in the Culture: The Workbook

NAME OF THE STORY: _____

Date read/ Screened

Story medium
(book, short story, movie, etc)

MEMBERS PRESENT FOR DISCUSSION

_____   _____

_____   _____

_____   _____

_____   _____

DISCUSSION **QUESTIONS**

1. In light of what was discussed about genres in *The Cross in the Culture*, does anything about this story stand out differently to you?

The Cross in the Culture: The Workbook

_____
_____
_____

2. What are some major world events currently unfolding in the news? In what ways do these events either tie into the story or affect the way you think about the plot points, development, or specific story elements?

_____
_____
_____

3. What does this story reveal about basic longings of the human heart?

_____
_____
_____

4. In your opinion, how does this story tell the truth?

_____
_____

5. In your opinion, are there any ways in which this story does not tell the truth?

6. If the storyteller were sitting here among you, what questions would you ask? What praise would you offer? What pushback?

7. Does the story give glory to the Triune God overtly or covertly? Describe how. Does this seem to be intentional on the storyteller's part?

The Cross in the Culture: The Workbook

8. Who in the story demonstrates actions or character qualities that remind you of Christ? of an anti-Christ?

   _____

   _____

   _____

9. What bridges can we build from this story to the gospel?

   _____

   _____

   _____

10. Are there any questions you would like to raise with the group?

    _____

    _____

    _____

The Cross in the Culture: The Workbook

NOTES

The Cross in the Culture: The Workbook

NAME OF THE STORY: _____

Date read/ Screened

Story medium
(book, short story, movie, etc)

MEMBERS PRESENT FOR DISCUSSION

_____   _____
_____   _____
_____   _____
_____   _____

DISCUSSION QUESTIONS

1. In light of what was discussed about genres in *The Cross in the Culture*, does anything about this story stand out differently to you?

The Cross in the Culture: The Workbook

_____

_____

_____

2. What are some major world events currently unfolding in the news? In what ways do these events either tie into the story or affect the way you think about the plot points, development, or specific story elements?

_____

_____

_____

3. What does this story reveal about basic longings of the human heart?

_____

_____

_____

4. In your opinion, how does this story tell the truth?

_____

_____

_____

The Cross in the Culture: The Workbook

5. In your opinion, are there any ways in which this story does not tell the truth? =

_____
_____
_____

6. If the storyteller were sitting here among you, what questions would you ask? What praise would you offer? What pushback?

_____
_____
_____

7. Does the story give glory to the Triune God overtly or covertly? Describe how. Does this seem to be intentional on the storyteller's part?

_____
_____
_____

8. Who in the story demonstrates actions or character qualities that remind you of Christ? of an anti-Christ?

The Cross in the Culture: The Workbook

_____

_____

_____

9. What bridges can we build from this story to the gospel?

_____

_____

_____

_____

_____

10. Are there any questions you would like to raise with the group?

_____

_____

_____

The Cross in the Culture: The Workbook

NOTES

The Cross in the Culture: The Workbook

NAME OF THE STORY: _____

Date read/ Screened

Story medium
(book, short story, movie, etc)

MEMBERS PRESENT FOR DISCUSSION

_____   _____

_____   _____

_____   _____

_____   _____

DISCUSSION **QUESTIONS**

1. In light of what was discussed about genres in *The Cross in the Culture*, does anything about this story stand out differently to you?

The Cross in the Culture: The Workbook

_____
_____
_____

2. What are some major world events currently unfolding in the news? In what ways do these events either tie into the story or affect the way you think about the plot points, development, or specific story elements?

_____
_____
_____

3. What does this story reveal about basic longings of the human heart?

_____
_____
_____

4. In your opinion, how does this story tell the truth?

_____
_____
_____

5. In your opinion, are there any ways in which this story does not tell the truth?

   _____
   _____
   _____

6. If the storyteller were sitting here among you, what questions would you ask? What praise would you offer? What pushback?

   _____
   _____
   _____

7. Does the story give glory to the Triune God overtly or covertly? Describe how. Does this seem to be intentional on the storyteller's part?

   _____
   _____
   _____

8. Who in the story demonstrates actions or character qualities that remind you of Christ? of an anti-Christ?

The Cross in the Culture: The Workbook

_____
_____
_____

9. What bridges can we build from this story to the gospel?

_____
_____
_____

10. Are there any questions you would like to raise with the group?

_____
_____
_____

The Cross in the Culture: The Workbook

NOTES

The Cross in the Culture: The Workbook

NAME OF THE STORY: _____

Date read/Screened

Story medium
(book, short story, movie, etc)

MEMBERS PRESENT FOR DISCUSSION

_____ _____

_____ _____

_____ _____

_____ _____

DISCUSSION **QUESTIONS**

1. In light of what was discussed about genres in *The Cross in the Culture*, does anything about this story stand out differently to you?

The Cross in the Culture: The Workbook

_____
_____
_____

2. What are some major world events currently unfolding in the news? In what ways do these events either tie into the story or affect the way you think about the plot points, development, or specific story elements?

_____
_____
_____

3. What does this story reveal about basic longings of the human heart?

_____
_____
_____

4. In your opinion, how does this story tell the truth?

_____
_____
_____

The Cross in the Culture: The Workbook

5. In your opinion, are there any ways in which this story does not tell the truth?

_____

_____

_____

6. If the storyteller were sitting here among you, what questions would you ask? What praise would you offer? What pushback?

_____

_____

_____

7. Does the story give glory to the Triune God overtly or covertly? Describe how. Does this seem to be intentional on the storyteller's part?

_____

_____

_____

8. Who in the story demonstrates actions or character qualities that remind you of Christ? of an anti-Christ?

The Cross in the Culture: The Workbook

_____
_____
_____

9. What bridges can we build from this story to the gospel?

_____
_____
_____
_____
_____

10. Are there any questions you would like to raise with the group?

_____
_____
_____

The Cross in the Culture: The Workbook

NOTES

The Cross in the Culture: The Workbook

NAME OF THE STORY: _____

| **Date read/ Screened** | **Story medium** (book, short story, movie, etc) |

MEMBERS PRESENT FOR DISCUSSION

_____   _____

_____   _____

_____   _____

_____   _____

DISCUSSION QUESTIONS

1. In light of what was discussed about genres in *The Cross in the Culture*, does anything about this story stand out differently to you?

The Cross in the Culture: The Workbook

_____

_____

_____

2. What are some major world events currently unfolding in the news? In what ways do these events either tie into the story or affect the way you think about the plot points, development, or specific story elements?

_____

_____

_____

3. What does this story reveal about basic longings of the human heart?

_____

_____

_____

4. In your opinion, how does this story tell the truth?

_____

_____

_____

5. In your opinion, are there any ways in which this story does not tell the truth?

   _____
   _____
   _____

6. If the storyteller were sitting here among you, what questions would you ask? What praise would you offer? What pushback?

   _____
   _____
   _____

7. Does the story give glory to the Triune God overtly or covertly? Describe how. Does this seem to be intentional on the storyteller's part?

   _____
   _____
   _____

8. Who in the story demonstrates actions or character qualities that remind you of Christ? of an anti-Christ?

The Cross in the Culture: The Workbook

_____

_____

_____

9. What bridges can we build from this story to the gospel?

_____

_____

_____

10. Are there any questions you would like to raise with the group?

_____

_____

_____

The Cross in the Culture: The Workbook

NOTES

The Cross in the Culture: The Workbook

NAME OF THE STORY: _____

Date read/ Screened

Story medium
(book, short story, movie, etc)

MEMBERS PRESENT FOR DISCUSSION

_____   _____
_____   _____
_____   _____
_____   _____

DISCUSSION **QUESTIONS**

1. In light of what was discussed about genres in *The Cross in the Culture*, does anything about this story stand out differently to you?

The Cross in the Culture: The Workbook

_____

_____

_____

2. What are some major world events currently unfolding in the news? In what ways do these events either tie into the story or affect the way you think about the plot points, development, or specific story elements?

_____

_____

_____

3. What does this story reveal about basic longings of the human heart?

_____

_____

_____

4. In your opinion, how does this story tell the truth?

_____

_____

_____

The Cross in the Culture: The Workbook

5. In your opinion, are there any ways in which this story does not tell the truth?

_____
_____
_____

6. If the storyteller were sitting here among you, what questions would you ask? What praise would you offer? What pushback?

_____
_____
_____

7. Does the story give glory to the Triune God overtly or covertly? Describe how. Does this seem to be intentional on the storyteller's part?

_____
_____
_____

8. Who in the story demonstrates actions or character qualities that remind you of Christ? of an anti-Christ?

The Cross in the Culture: The Workbook

_____
_____
_____

9. What bridges can we build from this story to the gospel?

_____
_____
_____

10. Are there any questions you would like to raise with the group?

_____
_____
_____

The Cross in the Culture: The Workbook

NOTES

The Cross in the Culture: The Workbook

NAME OF THE STORY: _____

| **Date read/ Screened** | **Story medium** *(book, short story, movie, etc)* |

MEMBERS PRESENT FOR DISCUSSION

_____   _____

_____   _____

_____   _____

_____   _____

DISCUSSION **QUESTIONS**

1. In light of what was discussed about genres in *The Cross in the Culture*, does anything about this story stand out differently to you?

The Cross in the Culture: The Workbook

_____

_____

_____

2. What are some major world events currently unfolding in the news? In what ways do these events either tie into the story or affect the way you think about the plot points, development, or specific story elements?

_____

_____

_____

3. What does this story reveal about basic longings of the human heart?

_____

_____

_____

4. In your opinion, how does this story tell the truth?

_____

_____

_____

The Cross in the Culture: The Workbook

5. In your opinion, are there any ways in which this story does not tell the truth?

_____

_____

_____

6. If the storyteller were sitting here among you, what questions would you ask? What praise would you offer? What pushback?

_____

_____

_____

7. Does the story give glory to the Triune God overtly or covertly? Describe how. Does this seem to be intentional on the storyteller's part?

_____

_____

_____

8. Who in the story demonstrates actions or character qualities that remind you of Christ? of an anti-Christ?

_____

The Cross in the Culture: The Workbook

_____

_____

9. What bridges can we build from this story to the gospel?

_____

_____

_____

10. Are there any questions you would like to raise with the group?

_____

_____

_____

The Cross in the Culture: The Workbook

NOTES

About the Author

Ruth Buchanan is a Christian writer who holds degrees in ministry and theology. She's traditionally published in the areas of fiction, non-fiction, plays, and sacred scripts. Though usually clamped to the keyboard, Ruth is also an eager reader, an enthusiastic traveler, and the world's most reluctant runner. She serves as Director of Literary Services for *Build a Better Us*.

. . .

Connect with Ruth on Social Media
Twitter: @RuthMBuchanan | Instagram: @RuthMBuchanan
www. RuthBuchananAuthor.com

Connect with Build a Better Us
Facebook: facebook.com/bbusocial/ | Twitter: @buildabtetterus Instagram: @bbusocial
www.buildabetterus.com

WHAT TO READ NEXT
AVAILABLE NOW!

WWW.RUTHBUCHANANAUTHOR.COM

www.ingramcontent.com/pod-product-compliance
Lightning Source LLC
Chambersburg PA
CBHW021958290426
44108CB00012B/1120